GLASNOST AND PERESTROIKA

Nigel Hawkes

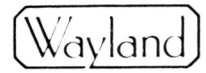

Wayland

World Issues

The Arms Trade
Cities in Crisis
Endangered Wildlife
The Energy Crisis
The Environment
The Exploitation of Space
Food or Famine?
Glasnost and Perestroika
Human Rights
The International Debt Crisis

The International Drugs Trade
International Terrorism
Nuclear Power
Nuclear Weapons
Population Growth
Refugees
Sport and Politics
Threatened Cultures
World Health

BORDERS REGIONAL LIBRARY	
ACCESSION No.	CLASS No.
V 10442	947.085

Cover: Gorbachov amongst the people.
Frontispiece: East meets West through gaps in the once impenetrable Berlin Wall.

Editor: Janet De Saulles
Series Designer: David Armitage

First published in 1990 by
Wayland (Publishers) Ltd.,
61, Western Road, Hove, BN3 1JD, England

© Copyright 1990 Wayland (Publishers) Ltd.

British Library Cataloguing In Publication Data
Hawkes, Nigel
  Glasnost and perestroika.
  (World issues)
  1. Soviet Union, 1982–
  I. Title II. Series
  947.0854

  ISBN 1 85210 865 7

Typeset by Nicola Taylor, Wayland
Printed by Rotolito Lombarda S.p.A., Italy
Bound by A.G.M. France

Contents

1. Introduction — 6
2. A nation in crisis — 12
3. Perestroika — 19
4. Glasnost — 27
5. The new thinking — 34
6. The Soviet empire — 38

Glossary — 46

Books to read — 47

Further information — 47

Index — 48

1 Introduction

way, the dictatorship of the proletariat of which Marx had dreamed was transformed into the dictatorship of a few individuals who claimed to act on the proletariat's behalf. Lenin declared, 'When we are reproached for exercising the dictatorship of a party, we say, 'Yes, the dictatorship of a party! We stand by it and cannot do without it'.'

The Soviet Union and Marx

In October 1917, in the midst of war and confusion, the Bolshevik Party seized power in Russia. At its head was the revolutionary Vladimir Ilyich Lenin. Tough, intelligent and single-minded, Lenin did not seek the consent of the Russian people in becoming their leader: he took advantage of a chaotic situation and organized an insurrection. The provisional government was not strong enough to put the Bolsheviks down by force and was overcome. It was less of a revolution than a *coup d'etat*.

Lenin was a socialist whose ideas were based on the works of Karl Marx, the nineteenth century German philosopher who had lived much of his life in London. Marx observed the miseries the Industrial Revolution had imposed on working people and concluded that conditions would not be improved until the proletariat, the working class, took power into its own hands. Marx believed that revolution would come in advanced societies where capitalism was furthest developed.

Like Marx, Lenin accepted that the people of Russia were not ready for a socialist revolution, seeing also that his Bolshevik Party was hardly better prepared to lead one. He believed that a small group of professional conspirators educated in revolutionary doctrine should direct events. He would lead, and the party would back him up, acting as a disciplined vanguard for socialism. In this

The revolutionary Bolshevik Party was inspired by Karl Marx. Marx himself thought it unlikely that Russia would follow the path he had mapped out.

The structure of Soviet power

In the USA, or other non-Communist countries, the systems of values and beliefs developed organically over a period of time. In the Soviet Union, however, the system known as Communism was imposed from above. Where Marx had dreamt of the liberation of the proletariat through its own actions, in the Soviet Union supreme power was placed in the hands of the few, and almost any means used to exercise that power was justified. From this time, power in the Soviet state rested not in the hands of the Prime Minister, or the president, but with the leader of the ruling party, the Bolsheviks, who in 1918 changed their name and became known as the Communist Party.

While the Bolshevik stage of the revolution had a relatively terror-free start, the

Workers and peasants joined in and supported the Russian Revolution.

increasing pace of the opposition led to the setting up in 1918 of the Extraordinary Commission to Combat Counter-Revolution and Sabotage (CHEKA). It was better, Lenin said, to 'discuss with rifles' than to engage in argument with his opponents. When workers failed to work, he advocated shooting one in ten of them on the spot in order to terrorize the others. A powerful force of secret policemen, today called the KGB, was formed to detect and harass dissidents and to impose the will of the Party on the people.

The structure created by Lenin survives in today's Soviet Union. When Lenin died in 1924, he was succeeded as General Secretary by Joseph Stalin, despite the fact that in a postscript to his Testament (will),

Lenin had denounced Stalin's ruthlessness. Once in power, Stalin took upon himself the task of recreating society from top to bottom. In so doing, he destroyed whole groups of people and expanded the power of the state to a degree unprecedented in history. Anybody who opposed Stalin was either shot or imprisoned. Huge numbers died in the forced collectivization of agriculture, in which small farmers were eliminated in favour of large collective farms. A modern Soviet demographer has estimated that in the period between 1931 and 1933 more than 9.4 million people died, most of these deaths being a result of famine deliberately created by Stalin to force change on the reluctant peasants. The total number of Stalin's victims will never be known, but it was certainly not less than 20 million, and may be as high as 40 million. Without much question, Stalin was the greatest mass murderer in history.

Stalin became General Secretary in 1924. The Soviet Union that Stalin took over was comprised of huge areas of undeveloped land, inhabited by many cultures.

Years after the purges of Stalin, Soviets still mourn the death of the thousands killed during his rule.

The changing face of the Soviet Union

Stalin's achievement, bought at the cost of so much blood, was to turn the Soviet Union into an industrialized country. Huge investments in steel, in mining, in heavy industry and in transport, all imposed by central dictat, transformed the country. Millions of peasants moved to the towns and became industrial workers. The economy, always in need of help and later crippled by the First World War and the chaos of revolution, now began to grow. When Nazi Germany declared war on the Soviet Union in 1941, defeat stared Stalin in the face. But the huge factories he had built, and the fortitude of the Russian people, eventually triumphed over Hitler. Victory in the Second World War, or the 'Great Patriotic War' as the Russians call it, was later used as another justification of all that Stalin had done to reshape Soviet society. 'Our people routed fascism with the might created by them in the 1920s and 1930s', Mikhail Gorbachov himself has written. 'Had there been no industrialization, we would have been unarmed before fascism.'

Brezhnev and Nixon worked towards better superpower relations, called détente.

Yet when Stalin died, it was not long before he was denounced. In a famous speech addressed to the twentieth Party Congress in 1956, the new leader, Nikita Khrushchev, recited a long catalogue of Stalin's sins. The indictment presented by Khrushchev was so damning that it was made available only to the inner circle of the Party: ordinary people were not allowed to read it until it was finally published in 1988. Khrushchev was an ambitious reformer who tried hard to decentralize the Soviet economy and radically change agricultural policy. These movements towards change, however, antagonized the Party and Khrushchev was overthrown by it in 1964.

His successor was Leonid Brezhnev. He was no liberal, and the cultural and social reforms begun by Khrushchev were soon abandoned. Millions remained imprisoned in labour camps, but Brezhnev did not return to the murderous policies of Stalin. In the early Brezhnev years attempts were made to encourage greater enterprise in Soviet industry. These had little real effect.

One of the main legacies left from the Brezhnev years was the intensification of conflict between the USA and the Soviet Union. This conflict, known as the Cold War, was one of ideologies, of competing political and economic systems and rival power-blocs of nations. It was a struggle between capitalism and communism.

The term 'Cold War' describes a situation where relations between East and West are not warm or easy but are cold. The term also has an opposite meaning: relations between East and West have not heated up to the point where war has broken out.

Within the framework of the Cold War, however, there were many armed confrontations in various parts of the world. The Cuban crisis of 1962 stepped up international tension between the USA and the Soviet Union and brought the world to the brink of a nuclear war. At this stage the

USA was ahead of the Soviet Union in its nuclear capacity. Following the US support of the invasion of Cuba in 1961, the Soviets placed nuclear weapons in Cuba itself, strategically making use of their more limited nuclear resources. The USA also intervened in Vietnam, increasing tension further. Under Brezhnev, the Soviets built up their stock of nuclear weapons in the attempt of maintaining a balance of power.

When Brezhnev died in 1982, the ageing Party stalwarts left behind opted for a reformer, Yuri Andropov, as his successor. But he lived for only another year, and was succeeded by an equally old and ill man, Konstantin Chernenko. When he, too, died after only a short period in office, the Politburo – the Party's ruling group – made a bold choice for his successor. They chose a man much younger than themselves, unsullied by the Stalin years, and committed to comprehensive reform. His name was Mikhail Gorbachov.

> 'Present-day conditions [demand] either peaceful coexistence or the most destructive war in history. There is no third way...The method of negotiation must become the sole method of solving international problems.'
> *Khrushchev, February 1956.*

Gorbachov's task is the increasingly difficult one of reforming his nation whilst, so far as possible, keeping it intact.

2 A nation in crisis

The Soviet Union that Gorbachov inherited on 11 March 1985 was a nation of bewildering contrasts. On the one hand the Soviet Union was leading in space exploration, and it had achieved a nuclear balance with the USA which made it a superpower. On the other hand there was mounting evidence of economic failure and social demoralization, concealed as much as possible from the outside world and the Soviet population itself by an obsessive secrecy. Even at the very top, few people knew how bad things were.

The Soviet economy

The centrally-planned economy created by Stalin had achieved some real successes. The Soviet Union is a huge country, with enormous resources and a large rural population. It did not need to import raw materials from abroad and it had no need to export finished products either. It could set its own standards and its own pace. Stalin threw all the national effort into the heavy industries. These expanded rapidly and by 1939 the Soviet Union was the biggest producer in Europe of oil, tractors and machine tools, and second in the world. In steel, cast iron, aluminium and electricity generation it was second in Europe, and third in the world, and in coal and cement it was third in Europe and fourth in the world. A nation that in 1917 had only recently begun to industrialize had built 99 blast furnaces, 391 open hearth furnaces, 207 electrical furnaces

The Titanium Space Obelisk, Moscow, is an inspiring monument to the Soviet Union's past and present achievements in space exploration.

and 227 rolling mills by 1939. Not for nothing had Stalin, born Joseph Djugashvili, adopted a name that means 'man of steel'.

By the 1970s, however, growth began to falter. Central planning that had proved adequate for the development of heavy industries was poorly adapted to the new industries which were flourishing in the USA and Japan, based as they were on high technology. By the 1980s, it was the number of computers, not the number of rolling mills, that gave the proper measure of an economy. In 1983 the USA had 96,500 large and medium computers in operation, Europe 23,400, Japan 16,900, and the Soviet Union only 3,040.

In addition, the quality of goods produced in the Soviet Union is poor, while Soviet agriculture is in even worse shape than Soviet industry. Although the country is vast and much of the soil fertile, the Soviet Union imports more than $15 billion worth of food every year. Peasants with no personal interest in the land have been forced to work in a system which offers them no satisfaction and few rewards. As

The Soviet Union has concentrated on the heavy industries, but if it is to compete successfully with countries such as the USA and Japan, it must continue to invest more in new technology.

a result, production of basic foods has never kept up with demand. Better results could be achieved: private allotments occupy only 3 per cent of the land area of the Soviet Union, yet produce 25 per cent of the food.

Statistics tell a grim story. Aleksandr Zaichenko, an economist writing in *Moscow News* in 1988, concluded that in terms of

'What an incredible picture! We have a total of 6,500 loss-making collective and state farms over the country as a whole. They hold 21 per cent of the arable land, 18 per cent of the pasture. Can you see, comrades, what is going on?' *Mikhail Gorbachov, speaking in October 1988 at a Kremlin meeting to discuss agriculture.*

per capita consumption of goods and services, the Soviet Union lies between fiftieth and sixtieth in the world league. Male life expectancy actually declined from an average of 66 years to 62 years during the Brezhnev rule. About 6 million citizens live in accommodation officially categorized as dangerous, and 50 million live in towns and cities where pollution levels go beyond even the generous Soviet norms. The Soviet Union has fewer metalled roads than India, and half the schools do not have central heating, running water or a sewerage system.

Until recently, Soviet spokespeople invariably asserted that inflation was impossible under Communism, and that the state budget balanced. This, they claimed, was in contrast to the large budget deficit built up by the USA. But in 1989 it was finally admitted that the Soviet Union does have a deficit, and an enormous one – 312 billion roubles. The deficit for 1989 alone is 120 billion roubles, equivalent to 13.8 per cent of the gross national product (GNP), while the US deficit represents only 3-4 per cent of its much larger GNP. Not surprisingly, the result of this large deficit is inflation, estimated at 10-11 per cent a year.

As if these were not problems enough, Gorbachov also has to deal with the social tensions created by economic failure and Stalinist repression. The Soviet Union is not a single nation, but an empire, created first by the tsars and later by the Communists. Officially it consists of fifteen separate republics, but within the largest of these, the Russian Soviet Federated Socialist Republic (RSFSR), are dozens of autonomous republics within which many different peoples live. The Soviet Union, it has been said, is a continent almost as large and certainly as varied as Africa.

Below *The Kremlin: in early 1990 Gorbachov announced that future governments would be elected through a multi-party system.*

Opposite *Eastern Europe, the Soviet Union and its republics. Today, the Eastern bloc is breaking up, and many republics are demanding independence.*

SOVIET UNION
RUSSIA
Leningrad
Moscow
ESTONIA
LATVIA
LITHUANIA
BYELORUSSIA
UKRAINE
MOLDAVIA
KAZAKHSTAN
Aral Sea
UZBEKISTAN
KIRGHIZIA
TADZHIKISTAN
TURKMENIA
Caspian Sea
AZERBAIJAN
GEORGIA
ARMENIA
Nagorno Karabakh
Black Sea
Baltic Sea
E.GERMANY
POLAND
CZECHOSLOVAKIA
HUNGARY
ROMANIA
YUGOSLAVIA
BULGARIA
ALBANIA
Mediterranean Sea

The rise of Gorbachov

The man entrusted by the Politburo with the task of finding answers to this network of interlocking problems was born on 2 March 1931 in the village of Privol'noye, in Stavropol, a fertile corner of the North Caucasus between the Volga and Don rivers. His parents were peasants, and his father became one of the first tractor drivers in the region. Both his father and grandfather were Party members. We do not know whether he has any brothers or sisters.

Having been a pupil at local schools, working on the farms in the summer as an assistant combine harvester operator, Gorbachov joined the Communist Party at the first possible opportunity. The same year, 1950, he won a place at Moscow State University, a considerable achievement for a boy from a provincial background. He studied law, a curious choice at the

Russian schoolgirl, Katya Lycheva, sends paper doves to US children as part of an exchange scheme, run in 1983 and 1986. The scheme was set up by the Soviet Union to improve contacts with the West.

time because the status of lawyers in Stalin's day was low. According to those who knew him at the time, Gorbachov studied hard, was loyal and honest and possessed a natural air of authority. His ideas appear to have been perfectly orthodox. When he graduated he went back to Stavropol to a job in the Party's youth wing, the Komsomol. Here he helped both to organize political education through lectures and publications, and to provide more traditional youth club activities such as sports meetings and summer camps.

Within a year after his return to Stavropol, Gorbachov had been made First Secretary of the city Komsomol committee. At about the same time he married Raisa Titorenko, also from Stavropol and a fellow student at Moscow State University. She had studied philosophy and it seems likely that the two had met in Moscow. Their only child, a daughter called Irina, was born the same year, 1956.

As First Secretary, Gorbachov was able to attend the twenty-second Party Congress. This was held in Moscow in 1961 and it was here that Khrushchev and others made open criticisms of Stalin's rule. After the congress was over, Stalin's body was removed from the mausoleum in Red Square where it had lain alongside Lenin's, and statues of Stalin were demolished throughout the Soviet Union. It was the high watermark of Khrushchev's liberalism, and a formative moment in Gorbachov's life.

Gorbachov realized, though, that the Komsomol offered no career for an ambitious man. In 1962 he found he was able to shift to full-time Party work. He became Party organizer in one of the sixteen agricultural units in the Stavropol area, and to learn more about the subject Gorbachov enrolled in a correspondence course at the Stavropol Agricultural Institute.

1975 saw yet another bad harvest in the Soviet Union. This photograph shows bulldozers clearing bushes and thin forest from the still-virgin lands near Minsk, in an effort to increase the area under cultivation of the Novoye Polesye State Farm.

Gorbachov now rose swiftly, first becoming secretary of the Stavropol region party. In 1978 he moved to Moscow to become secretary of the Party Central Committee responsible for agriculture. In this job, he was no more successful than any of his predecessors, and a series of poor harvests threatened his future. He was not personally responsible for the failures, which resulted from the basic structure of Soviet agriculture, but as the man in charge he was the one to be blamed. When the 1982 harvest fell short, this time forcing the Soviet Union to import millions of tonnes of grain, Gorbachov must have been worried. But fate stepped in and saved him. Just a week before the Party met to discuss the harvest, Brezhnev died from a heart attack. Gorbachov's supporter, Yuri Andropov, took over, and the blame for failure was diverted from Gorbachov on to the shoulders of the dead General Secretary.

Under Andropov, Gorbachov had nothing to fear, even though the agricultural problem got no better. But Andropov's death from kidney failure on 9 February 1984 came too early for Gorbachov. He did not have the seniority to succeed, and had to sit by while the Politburo elected Konstantin Chernenko, a nonentity best known for having been Brezhnev's secretary. Chernenko was already ill with the lung disease emphysema when he was elected, so perhaps Gorbachov did not feel too disappointed: during Chernenko's ineffective reign Gorbachov became, in effect, his deputy. In December he visited London, impressing everybody with his easy manner, intelligence and good sense of humour.

Soon, Chernenko was in palpable decline, and the Politburo was ready to nominate Gorbachov as his successor. When Chernenko finally died on 9 March 1985, there was no delay. Despite an attempt to put up a rival candidate, Gorbachov was swiftly elected leader. He was just 54, a young man in comparison with those who had been running the Soviet Union for the previous decade. He was attractive and quick-witted, popular both at home and abroad. If anybody stood a chance of solving the Soviet Union's problems, this was the man.

Chernenko was already seriously ill when he was chosen to lead the Soviet Union. Gorbachov acted as unofficial deputy during Chernenko's short period of power.

'We are now like a seriously ill man who, after a long time in bed, takes his first step with the greatest difficulty and finds, to his horror, that he has almost forgotten how to walk.' *Economist Nikolai Shmelyev, writing in Novy Mir, spring 1987.*

3 Perestroika

The role of state planning

In the Soviet Union, everything operates according to a plan. Karl Marx believed that private enterprise led to exploitation, and free markets to anarchy. He wanted the production of goods 'to be regulated by society'. In the Soviet Union his ideas came into being, leading to some unexpected results.

The power to determine who produces what lies in the hands of Gosplan, the State Planning Commission. It sends out quarterly, half-yearly and yearly plans to every enterprise in the Soviet Union, telling them what raw materials they will get, and what they must turn them into. A factory that meets its targets is awarded with bonuses; those who consistently fail are in trouble.

The greatest weakness of the Plan — for it is so important it deserves a capital letter — is that it can measure only quantity, not quality. It can order a factory producing men's suits to make 250,000 of them, and arrange for it to be supplied with the necessary cloth, thread, buttons, zips, sewing machines, and labour (no simple task in itself), but it cannot ensure that the suits are fit to wear. So long as the manager produces the right number of suits, he or she is in the clear. If they pile up in the shops because nobody wants to buy them, that is somebody else's problem

The tyranny of the Plan explains much about the Soviet economy. It explains why managers are so reluctant to use new technology: to shift from well-established methods is to risk not meeting the Plan's targets. It also explains why productivity is so low: managers like to hang on to workers, even if they are doing nothing, just in case there is a sudden need to increase output to meet the Plan. It has been estimated that it takes seven Soviet factory workers to do the work done by one in the USA. It even explains why Soviet medicines are often useless: in order to meet the Plan, or even exceed it, drug factories will sometimes dilute the medicines and pills they make. A Soviet doctor who emigrated to Israel says, 'When we saw a medicine that had no effect, we often said 'That must be above-Plan production'.'

In a simple economy, the Plan worked tolerably well. But today's world is different. Leonid Abalkin, Director of the Institute of Economics at the USSR Academy of Sciences, puts it this way: 'The industrial situation of the 1930s differs from the technological situation of the late 1980s. We can catch up with, and even overtake, other countries by 'crude iron', without intellect, without virtuosity, just by sheer enthusiasm and physical strength. But at present, there is a vertical, not horizontal, gap between our country and other industrial states — a gap in education and culture, just like a gap in epochs. You will not be able to cross it in one jump.'

Some new solutions

By the time Gorbachov came to power, the problems of the centrally-planned, 'command' economy were apparent to everybody. His first instinct was to apply traditional remedies, much like those attempted by Andropov two years earlier.

> 'One is lucky to find only string, sand, or small nails in a Moscow sausage.'
> A reporter from Literaturnya Gazeta visiting a sausage factory.

Until recently stalls such as these ones, set up for May Day celebrations, were not allowed to sell alcohol.

He called for harder work, greater discipline, more quality control. He also urged an acceleration of the production of consumer goods and the use of new technology by industry.

More original, though no more popular, was Gorbachov's campaign against vodka. Heavy drinking has always been a problem in the Soviet Union, but by the 1980s alcoholism was rife. Its damaging effects on health, family life and industrial productivity are enormous.

Used by many to blot out the realities of a hard and unrewarding life, vodka is responsible for the high figures in crime, absenteeism, abandoned children, the increase in road accidents and a reduced life expectancy. Gorbachov's answer was to issue a series of decrees that increased penalties for drunkenness, reduced the number of shops selling vodka, and made it an offence to supply drink to young people. It was a deeply unpopular campaign, and only partly successful. Lives were saved, but many people simply spent yet longer in queues to buy their vodka, or turned to home distilling, causing a run on sugar that left the shelves bare. Moreover, the state lost the profits on vodka, amounting to 7 per cent of its revenues, which precipitated a budget crisis. Today the strict laws have largely been dropped.

It soon became clear that exhortation and sobriety were not enough. Beginning in 1986, a radical new policy, called perestroika (restructuring) was launched. Its aim was a major overhaul of the Soviet economy. To achieve it Gorbachov was willing to incorporate some of the ideas that make Western economies work. Factories would be allowed much more freedom to make their own decisions, and management would become directly accountable to workers; thousands of loss-making enterprises (one in three farms and one in eight factories) would be wound up and privately-owned businesses and co-operatives would be encouraged. A new law would allow foreign companies to invest in joint ventures with Soviet enterprises. These would be outside the control of Gosplan, and the foreign companies would be allowed to take the bulk of any profits home. Furthermore, Soviet organizations would be allowed to export goods, at prices set by them, and retain any hard currency earnings to spend as they wished. They would even be able to lend such earnings to other Soviet enterprises. This broke the monopoly of the Ministry for Foreign Trade for the first time since it was established by Lenin.

A. Stroyer, chief of the Main Moscow's Civil Engineering Department and P. Word, president of a US firm, shake hands at the 'Stroidormash' 88 international exhibition. The Soviet-US venture includes the construction and repair of buildings.

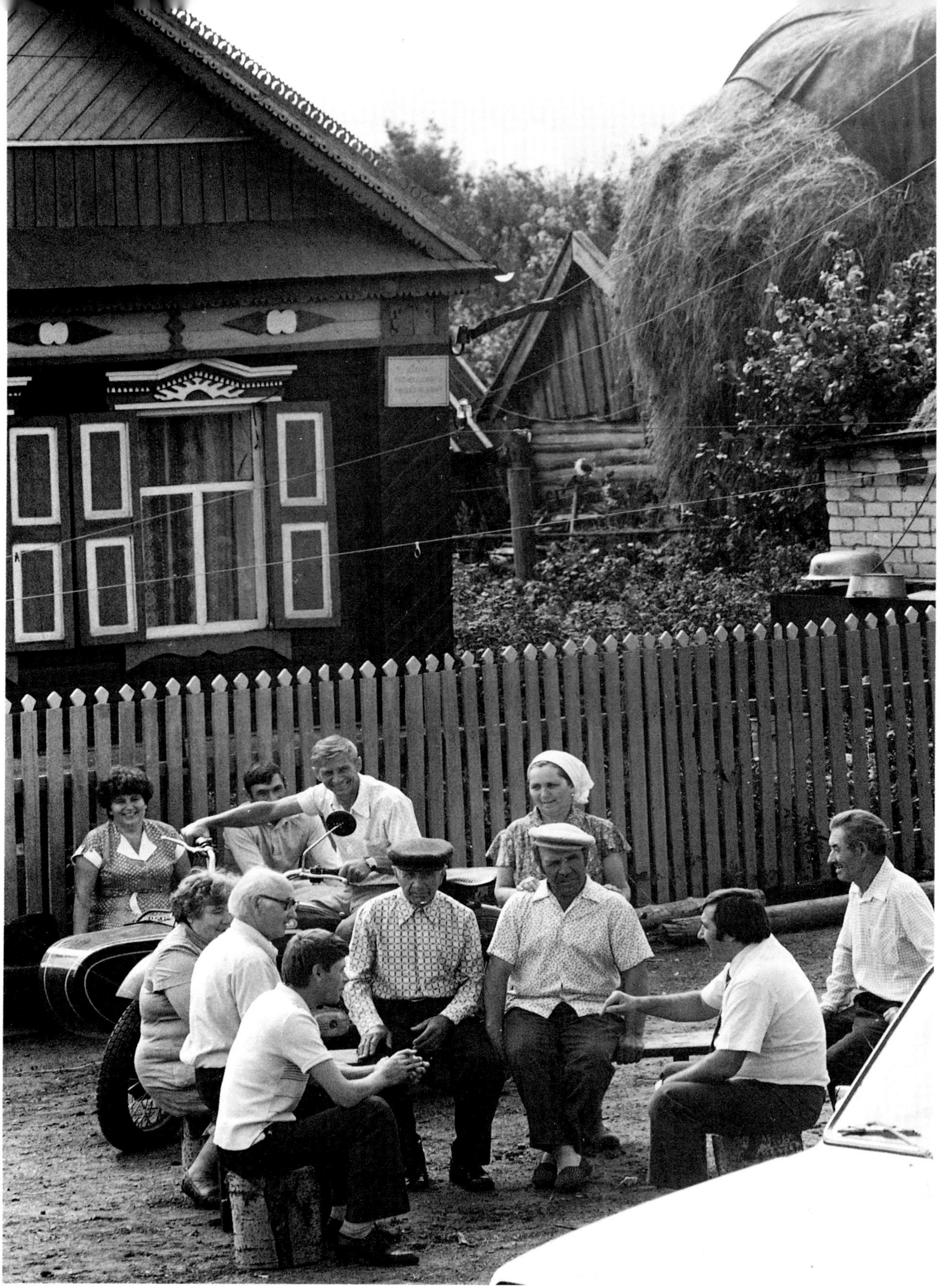

Agriculture and perestroika

Perestroika also called for dramatic changes on the farms, which today consume one-third of all government spending. Gorbachov's first move, in November 1985, was to merge five existing ministries to form a 'superministry', Gosagraprom, the State Agro-Industrial Committee. Created in haste and with little discussion, Gosagraprom proved a complete failure, simply introducing even more layers of bureaucracy into the system. In March 1989, it was decided that it should be dissolved. This is the first recorded instance of Gorbachov being forced to reform his own reforms.

Much more positive was Gorbachov's permissive attitude towards the private ownership of land. Although small private plots are invariably far more productive than the huge collective farms, they have always been frowned upon as evidence of a retreat from socialism and a move towards capitalism. Gorbachov attacked this attitude strongly: 'What kind of private entrepreneurial activity can it be when the family is working its own small garden, spending its time out of doors?' he demanded. 'So we have now taken the decision to allocate annually from 1 million to 1¼ million allotments to citizens.'

In 1989 he went even further, opening up the possibility of a return to private agriculture, by making land available to tenant farmers. The state would continue to own it, but the tenants would have sufficient security of tenure to make it worthwhile to farm properly and look after the land, just as tenant farmers do in Western Europe. In August 1989, in order to encourage farmers, the government announced that in future they would be paid partly in foreign currencies rather than solely in roubles.

Opposite *With Gorbachov's agricultural reforms, some farmers are beginning to prosper. Meetings such as this one are held to discuss surplus contracts.*

Reform: success or failure?

These are radical ideas by Soviet standards, but their effect on industry and food supply has so far been modest. In Moscow today you can dine at a private enterprise restaurant, call a private taxi, take your car to a private garage or hire a private translator – all things that would have been impossible a few years ago. Inside Soviet factories and farms, however, less has changed. The system has proved a tough opponent, blunting the drive for reform before it could ever properly get under way.

Above *In March 1990, the Congress of People's Deputies elected Gorbachov President of the USSR, giving him sweeping executive powers.*

The case of Alim Chabanov illustrates the difficulties of perestroika. He was dismissed from his director's duties and expelled from the Communist Party when his company produced machine-tools without the official forms.

The first defeat came in June 1987, when the Law on State Enterprises was published. It failed to tackle the problems of bankruptcy, or price reform. The idea of 20 million people losing their jobs with the closure of loss-making enterprises, combined with a doubling of food prices, frightened the Politburo. Although Gorbachov himself has said that 'without reform of prices, the economic reform will make no progress', the actual measures were put off until 1990 and 1991. At present, food prices are still very low, too low to encourage farmers. Because they are so low, a lot of food produce is wasted: bread is often bought to feed animals, or cheap meat is fed to rabbits whose skins make the much-prized Russian fur hat. One of the main obstacles to price reform has always been that Soviet citizens are used to subsidized food and regard it as a disaster when they have to pay market prices.

A second failure for reform came when the leadership insisted that economic 'acceleration' should continue alongside perestroika, and that the optimistic goals of the current Five-Year Plan should still be met. This left a lot of power in the hands of the central planners. They were still able to impose their targets, even on enterprises which were theoretically free to make their own decisions. The result, in the words of Ivan Laptev, the editor of *Izvestia*, was 'an astonishing, unique situation: the person who makes the decisions (an official of the Communist Party) bears no legal or material responsibility for its consequences, and the person who bears that responsibility (the factory manager) does not make the decisions'.

One of the greatest problems the factory managers face is their powerlessness to set prices or negotiate wages. As both are centrally determined, any incentive to keep costs down or to try to make a profit is removed. Factory managers simply do not know whether their enterprises are profitable or not. And the industrial ministries, which ought to know, have shied away from the promise to close down the loss-makers because of fears of social unrest. The more energetic managers are using the new freedoms to improve their factories, but there is not very much they can do. The lazier ones – the majority – prefer to continue doing what Gosplan and the ministries say. They know that nobody ever got sacked in the Soviet Union for doing as he or she was told.

Perestroika has not benefitted everyone. For these Muscovites, the standard of living remains the same.

Living standards

One of the major architects of perestroika, Gorbachov's economic adviser Abel Aganbegyan, rashly promised in December 1987 that 'the first thing perestroika will bring will be an improvement in living standards'. So far, it has signally failed to do this. The evidence is that the decline in living standards is continuing, and that people are beginning to lose faith in perestroika. The problem is that the costs of reform – price rises, redundancies, loss of bonuses because of tighter quality control – are immediately visible, while the benefits – higher incomes and more consumer goods – are just promises that may never materialize. Opinion polls show that only 30-40 per cent of the public are in favour of perestroika.

In July 1989, the growing unrest broke out in a series of strikes by miners that sent a chill through the Kremlin. Strikes are almost unknown in the Soviet Union, though not illegal; in the past they have been put down with force. But the Siberian miners who went on strike in the Kuzbass Basin, a dirty, dreary region polluted by years of heavy industry and lack of care, got everything they asked for: more pay, better working conditions, and improved supplies of food. As the strikes began to spread, similar concessions were offered to miners in the Ukraine, in the far north and in Central Asia.

The strikes broke out with bewildering speed. They began when 77 miners walked off the job in the Kuzbass. The next day, 11 July, 12,000 followed them, and at the height of the disturbances 300,000 workers paralyzed 250 mines. In huge demonstrations in nine cities, they held up placards declaring: DOWN WITH BUREAUCRATS and KUZBASS: CLEAN AIR, MEAT FOR EVERYONE, WE DEMAND SOCIAL JUSTICE. Miners complained that when they came up after six hours underground, they could not even find a bar of soap to wash with. The ration provides them with only one bar every two months.

Gorbachov showed his usual political skill in presenting the strikes as a gesture of support for perestroika and against the

Deaths in the mining community due to poor working conditions led to strikes in the Kuzbass Basin. The Siberian miners managed to win all their demands.

bureaucrats who in his view are blocking its progress. But the real message was alarming: unless perestroika can begin to deliver the economic benefits it has promised, the workforce will use the new freedoms Gorbachov has given them to cause a lot of trouble. The pay increases for the Kuzbass alone will cost the coal industry over $100 million. Gorbachov was also forced to promise 6,600 tonnes of meat, 10,160 tonnes of sugar and more consumer goods in the shops. The Soviet system is neither strong enough nor rich enough to survive if workers everywhere rise up and demand what the Siberian miners won.

'It must be said frankly, comrades – we underestimated the depths and gravity of the distortions and stagnations of the past. There was a lot we just didn't know, and are seeing only now. It turned out that neglect was more serious than we thought.'
Mikhail Gorbachov to the Communist Party Conference, summer 1989.

4 Glasnost

The most dramatic change in the Soviet Union since 1985 has been in what can be said and what can be written. Suddenly, the truth is being told. The things that Soviets have always discussed privately, sitting around a table in their kitchens late at night over interminable cups of tea, are now being said openly at meetings of the People's Congress and the Supreme Soviet. History is being rewritten. Books long proscribed are being published and widely read. The deepest feelings of the oppressed minorities in an empire ruled by Russians are finding expression. It is all astonishingly new and refreshing, like a window being flung open on a room full of stale air and dusty relics of the past.

New freedoms

These changes have been made possible by Gorbachov's policy of glasnost or 'openness'. The word means more than simply freedom of speech, although it includes that. It also means the obligation of the Party and the bureaucracy to be open in their decision-making, to respond to criticism, and to listen to advice. Glasnost, Gorbachov has said, 'means pluralism of views on any issues of domestic and foreign policy, free comparison of different opinions, and discussion.' Without it, he told the nineteenth Party Conference in June 1988, there can be no renovation of Soviet society, no chance to create a new moral atmosphere in which to push the ideas of perestroika forward.

Plays, which before glasnost would never have been shown, are now freely performed. This photograph shows a scene from the controversial 'Dictatorship of Conscience' written by Y. Shatrov.

Glasnost is combined with a second policy, equally revolutionary: demokratizatsiya or democratization. For 70 years, Soviet citizens have been told what to do by leaders they did not elect and dared not criticize. In April 1989, freely contested elections were held for the Congress of People's Deputies. Given a chance to express their view in the first proper election since 1918 (where Lenin ignored the fact that the Bolsheviks lost), the people threw out a number of unpopular Party functionaries. In their place they elected some independent and critical voices, including the foremost dissident of the Brezhnev years, Andrei Sakharov, and the radical populist Boris Yeltsin, sacked from the Politburo for his outspokenness eighteen months earlier. The Congress met in May, and in an electrifying series of meetings shown on TV and broadcast on the radio, the new members expressed their conflicting views in an atmosphere of freedom not experienced since the revolution.

The third leg upon which Gorbachov's new society rests is the rule of law. During Stalin's era, the law became whatever the dictator wanted it to be. Any sense of using the law to protect the rights of individuals was eradicated. In a series of show trials in the 1930s, Stalin's opponents were forced to make humiliating confessions of their 'errors' before being led away to be shot. Because so many officials felt themselves to be, and indeed were, above the law, widespread corruption went unpunished. Under Khrushchev various legal reforms had taken place. The courts were not fully autonomous, but rulings began to be treated with respect and deference. With Gorbachov, the process is going yet further. A new legal code is being drafted which is designed to correct the balance between the state and the individual, guaranteeing the independence of courts and the supremacy of the law over and above Party and Soviet bureaucracy.

An increase in Western influence is another mark of glasnost. The first Soviet national beauty contest was held in 1989. Here, entrants in the elimination stage of the contest walk across Red Square.

Gorbachov and the media

The first beneficiaries of glasnost were the press and television. Under the old rules, news was tightly controlled by the Party. Every word that appeared in a Soviet newspaper had to pass the scrutiny of political censors, though editors themselves knew pretty well what they were allowed to say. It was not simply that criticism of the party was forbidden; railway accidents, industrial disasters and plane crashes were also taboo, because they implied that things were less than perfect in the Soviet Union. Drugs, prostitution, mental illness and pollution were also ignored, for the same reason. Novels are often serialized in the press, but it was impossible to publish books like Alexander Solzhenitsyn's *Gulag Archipelago*, a massive novel about Stalin's labour camps. Under the new rules, this book, long available in the West, is finally to be serialized for Soviet readers. Another novel about the Stalin years, Anatoli Rybakov's *Children of the Arbat*, has taken twenty years to be published but has already sold 5 million copies since 1987.

Two of the most liberal publications in the glasnost era are *Moscow News*, edited by Yegor Yakovlev, and the magazine *Ogonyok*, edited by Vitali Korotich. They have gone beyond criticism of the past, and are even prepared to publish articles and letters that cast doubt on perestroika itself.

This feeling that perestroika has not yet gone far enough is expressed in a joke. A visiting dog asks a Soviet dog what has changed under Gorbachov. 'Well, it's like this', says the Soviet dog. 'First they gave me a longer chain; but then they shifted my bowl out of reach. The main difference now is that I can bark as loud as I like.'

Among the new freedoms of the Soviet people is the right to demonstrate. These people are actively supporting this right stating, 'People elect the President' and 'Perestroika for the constitution'.

The huge success of *Ogonyok*, the circulation of which has risen from 300,000 at the beginning of 1986 to more than 3 million, proves that the public likes the sound of barking. But it also irritates many who grew up in the days of Soviet orthodoxy. A conservative backlash against the Gorbachov reforms has developed, both within the Party (which sees its traditional privileges being eroded) and among the general public. It was given dramatic expression in 1988 by Nina Andreyeva, a chemistry teacher at a Leningrad technical institute. She wrote a long article that appeared in the conservative daily *Sovietskaya Rossiya*. Perhaps significantly, her article appeared at a moment when Gorbachov was out of the country, and many believe its publication and its prominence were engineered by his main conservative opponent within the USSR's Politburo, Yegor Ligachov.

Describing herself as 'a true Communist', Andreyeva said that Stalin's purges 'were being blown out of proportion'. She added that had Gorbachov been a politician in the late 1920s, he would have been branded 'a right-wing deviationist' and they would have lined him up against a wall. 'Now right is left and left is right and no one knows what anything means any more. Who is who?' wrote Andreyeva.

'Throughout its history, the Soviet Union has not had a single civilized law, with the exception perhaps of the 1922 Civil Code, which we borrowed from pre-Revolutionary Russia.' *Sergei Alekseyev, Chairman of the Supreme Soviet Committee for Legislation, Legality, Law and Order, in an interview with Izvestia, July 1989.*

After Gorbachov's return, the official newspaper *Pravda* responded with an editorial denouncing Andreyeva's article as 'nostalgia, backward-looking patriotism' and claiming that it was an attempt to reverse Party policy on the sly. But Andreyeva was clearly not alone in holding the views she expressed. In the weeks following the publication of her article she received 7,000 letters of support.

Glasnost has provided many frustrated citizens with an opportunity to criticize. This entry in a contest entitled 'Perestroika and Ourselves', shows a canvas painted with an abundance of crops, standing in a barren field. The figure represents Gorbachov and the inscription reads 'Down with the empty show-off!'

What glasnost means for dissenters

Dissidents have also benefited enormously from the new climate. It has always taken great courage to speak out against the Party, and millions suffered imprisonment and death for doing so. Not for nothing did a pre-revolutionary Russian, Koz'ma Prutkov, remark: 'Think before you speak. Maybe you won't speak at all if you do.' Yet over the years there have been those who have dared to speak, foremost among them the late Andrei Sakharov, one of the physicists who developed the Soviet hydrogen bomb. In 1966, as an honoured and pampered member of the Soviet elite, he wrote to Brezhnev protesting at the arrest of four people who had themselves protested against the trial of two writers. In 1968 he was removed from secret work, and later he was banished to the closed city of Gorky, where foreigners are not allowed to travel. As a member of the Soviet Academy of Sciences, Sakharov enjoyed some degree of protection against the state, so he was never imprisoned. But his life was made as difficult as the authorities could contrive.

The popular television programme 'Before and After Midnight' is a product of glasnost. The presenter, Vladimir Molchanov, provides a combination of news, entertainment and political journalism.

Nobel prize winner Andrei Sakharov was a leading supporter of perestroika. He urged Gorbachov to go as fast as possible with his reforms, fearing for their success if too cautious a path was followed.

In December 1986, Sakharov was released from exile and allowed to come back to Moscow. In due course he was elected to the People's Congress, and there he continued to make speeches attacking the failings of the Soviet state. He was even allowed to travel abroad and make the same criticisms, an astonishing transformation which does Gorbachov enormous credit. Speaking at Harvard University in August 1989, Sakharov warned that Gorbachov was moving too slowly with perestroika. His approach could lead to economic or political disaster. 'If we allow this to go on, we are threatened with chaos,' the 68-year-old Soviet physicist warned. 'We may be threatened with a military coup. We may be threatened with famine.'

Sakharov, who died of heart failure in December 1989, was one of the members of a 400-strong group in the People's Congress who have called for speedier progress with perestroika. They are a minority in the 2,250-seat Congress and heavily outnumbered by the more orthodox majority. But even the existence of the group, which calls itself the 'Inter-Regional Group', is a challenge to authority. Ever since 1921, the Communist Party has banned members from forming factions which could challenge the line of the Party leader. Under Lenin the punishment for doing so was expulsion; under Stalin, the firing squad.

Boris Yeltsin, who believes in a faster pace for reforms than Gorbachov does, helps lead the newly-formed Democratic Platform.

A leading member of the group is Boris Yeltsin, who has rapidly emerged as the nearest thing the Soviet Union has to a leader of the opposition. Purged from the Politburo in 1987 in circumstances that still remain mysterious, after a speech in which he attacked the Party for dragging its heels over perestroika, Yeltsin has since become the darling of Moscow. Officially, he is still 'the leader who failed', but the Moscow electors gave a very different verdict when he stood for the People's Congress in April 1989 and romped home with 89 per cent of the vote. Part of his popularity is undoubtedly due to his attack on party privileges such as special shops, where all the delicacies denied to ordinary people are available for senior Party members.

> 'On the waves of perestroika, scum and rubbish have come to the surface.' *Yegor Ligachov, in a speech in Moscow, July 1989.*

Yeltsin's precise position is an interesting one. On the face of it, he is a strong supporter of Gorbachov, though urging him to go faster. Yet Gorbachov made no move to save him when he offended the Politburo and was sacked, or to help him when he sought rehabilitation at the Party conference in 1988. On that occasion Ligachov shouted 'You're wrong, Boris!' as Yeltsin made his speech. Yeltsin got his own back by issuing supporters in his election campaign with buttons that declared: 'Yegor, you're wrong!' The chances are that Gorbachov, trying to maintain Party unity over perestroika, finds the support of the outspoken Yeltsin something of an embarrassment. The need for Gorbachov to step carefully between the extreme left, including Yeltsin, and right-wing conservatives, such as Ligachov, becomes increasingly great. It is in this that Gorbachov's skills of leadership are tested to the limits.

Many figures who were defeated in the election lost even though they ran unopposed: to win they needed to gain at least 50 per cent of the poll. The entire five-man leadership in Leningrad, the top leadership in Lithuania, the Mayor of Moscow (who was seen as a party hatchet man), the head of the KGB in Estonia and the Mayor of Kiev were all defeated. The changes were particularly comprehensive in the Baltic republics of Estonia, Lithuania and Latvia, countries which were

> 'Could our perestroika be compared to an aircraft that has taken off without knowing if there is a landing strip at its destination?' *Yuri Bondarev, Deputy Chairman of the Writers' Union of the Russian Republic.*

Above *Like many other Soviet republics, Estonia is pressing for independence.*

Below *A Romanian prays for the victims of his country's struggle against dictatorship. Gorbachov supported the Romanian revolution, which overthrew Ceaucescu.*

incorporated into the Soviet state in 1940 after Stalin signed the notorious Nazi-Soviet Pact with Hitler.

The political freedom offered by Gorbachov has been seized by the Baltic states and by other minorities within the Soviet Union. A series of demonstrations and outbreaks of violence have occurred in Armenia, Azerbaijan, Georgia, Moldavia, Uzbekistan and even in the Ukraine, the latter perilously close to the Russian heartland. The ambition of the Baltic states is to secede from the Soviet Union. Others may try to take the same route, though their problems are more complex, resulting in many cases from the arbitrary way in which Stalin moved minority peoples around the map because of his doubts about their loyalty during the Second World War.

Glasnost and demokratizatsiya have allowed all these groups to find their voices again, and presented Gorbachov with yet another problem; the uprising of nationalist fervour from every corner of his far-flung empire.

5 The new thinking

> 'Force or the threat of force neither can, nor should be, instruments of foreign policy...our credo is as follows: political issues shall be resolved only by political means, and human problems only in a humane way.' *Mikhail Gorbachov, addressing the United Nations General Assembly, 7 December 1988.*

Foreign policy

Hand in hand with Gorbachov's domestic policy is his bold and revolutionary foreign policy. The changes that he has brought are greater than any since the days of Lenin, and have made him the best known and perhaps the most admired leader in the world today. One by one, the old ideas of Brezhnev and his successors have been abandoned in favour of Gorbachov's 'new thinking' – the equivalent of perestroika and glasnost in foreign policy. Such changes, as an American scholar has remarked, do not make states into saints, but they do create a vastly different challenge for the other nations of the world, one to which Western Europe and the USA have found it difficult to respond.

Gorbachov inherited a foreign policy mess almost as profound as his economic and political problems. Under Brezhnev, the Soviet Union had built up its armed forces, and taken a hand in many conflicts in the Developing Countries, while at the same time trying to maintain good relations with the West. Brezhnev believed that as Soviet power grew, the West would be forced to become more and more accommodating, reaching agreements with Moscow on trade, arms control and the transfer of technology. The opposite happened. Alarmed by the huge and growing Soviet forces, the West continued its own arms build-up and withdrew its co-operation on trade and technology. The policy of détente or relaxation, negotiated between Brezhnev and President Nixon in the early 1970s, was collapsing even before Soviet troops invaded Afghanistan in December 1979. The invasion appeared simply to confirm what many in the West believed about the Soviet Union: that it was a military power determined to achieve world domination.

In Europe, the North Atlantic Treaty Organization (NATO) responded to the Soviet missile build-up by deploying new weapons of its own: US-built cruise and Pershing-2 missiles which could strike at the Soviet heartland from bases in Britain, West Germany, Italy, Belgium and Holland. NATO offered to negotiate away these missiles before they had been deployed, if the Soviets would do the same. But in the autumn of 1983, the Soviet Union walked out of the talks. East-West relations had reached an impasse.

Gorbachov quickly recognized that Soviet policy was getting nowhere. Further, apart from wishing to reduce international tension, the Soviet Union has a vested interest in reducing arms

> 'We have managed to do away with the spirit of confrontation in international affairs, and change this into dialogue.' *Eduard Shevardnadze, in an interview in Argumenti i Fakty, May 1989.*

expenditure. With all the work and money to be spent on updating the Soviet Union's still backward economy, Gorbachov is in desperate need of extra revenue. In July 1985 Gorbachov replaced Andrei Gromyko, the world's longest serving Foreign Minister after twenty-eight years in office, with a man with a more flexible and open mind. Eduard Shevardnadze, a Georgian, had no experience of foreign policy but had been highly successful as Party boss in Georgia.

Gorbachov's new thinking is based on a few simple propositions. He argues that international security comes not from armed strength, but from political compromise, and that one nation cannot improve its own security by making another feel insecure. Human interests, above all the desire for peace, are more important than ideological concepts like the class struggle, or the war against imperialism. Nuclear wars cannot be won, and must not be fought. And finally, the problems of the Developing Countries are not part of a grand 'national liberation struggle' justifying Soviet involvement, but are a huge waste of scarce resources and a potential focus of international tension.

These are all radical ideas to come from a Soviet leader. Ever since the break up of the wartime alliance between the USA, Britain and the Soviet Union, relations between East and West have been portrayed by Soviet spokespeople as a clash of irreconcilable ideas. Gorbachov, by contrast, is now saying that foreign policy is not an ideological matter, and that flexibility and respect for the opinions of others will get better results.

'What we are witnessing in the Soviet Union are events no less fundamental and far-reaching than those which occurred in France in 1789.' *Professor Michael Howard, Professor of Modern History at Oxford, speaking at Chatham House, May 1989.*

Looking for a new policy towards the outside world, Gorbachov appointed Eduard Shevardnadze as Foreign Minister.

The USSR and international relations

The effects of the Soviet Union's new foreign policy have been dramatic. As Shevardnadze put it in an interview in May 1989: 'Our relations with the surrounding world are on a more even keel and have become calmer. We have strengthened our security, not by introducing new super-forces and more arms, but by introducing the right policy. Our country's international prestige has noticeably increased, as has trust in what we say and do.'

The concrete achievements have been many. Following the first meeting between Gorbachov and ex-President Reagan in Geneva in November 1985, an agreement was reached that will eliminate many of the nuclear missiles in Europe – the first time in history that a whole class of nuclear weapons will be scrapped. The two sides have also agreed in principle to cut their inter-continental missile forces by 50 per cent, though the details remain to be worked out.

In Vienna, talks have begun on sweeping reductions in conventional weapons, in which the Soviet Union has a clear advantage over the West. Success in those talks may allow further reductions in short-range nuclear weapons in Europe, as the Soviet Union has urged.

The Soviet Union withdrew its troops from Afghanistan in February 1989. The Afghan invasion, it was recognized, had taken place at heavy cost to the USSR.

The new thinking has also helped to ease other regional conflicts, most importantly in Angola, where a civil war has been raging between the Marxist government, supported by Cuba, and the UNITA rebels, who had the support of South Africa and the USA. In a complex negotiation organized by the USA, both South Africa and Cuba agreed to withdraw their troops from the country.

Gorbachov's diplomatic offensive has been carried to the West in a series of highly successful visits. In addition to the series of summit meetings with ex-President Reagan held in Geneva, Reykjavik, Moscow and Washington, Gorbachov has made trips to London, Bonn and Paris. While Western leaders are agreed that he should be encouraged, their degrees of enthusiasm vary. Mrs Thatcher likes him personally, but disagrees with him over nuclear weapons. While he dreams of a non-nuclear world, she argues that nuclear weapons are indispensable.

Chancellor Helmut Kohl of West Germany, and particularly his Foreign Minister, Hans-Dietrich Genscher, take a much less belligerent line. They would like NATO to agree to Soviet suggestions that all nuclear weapons in Europe be eliminated. So, the effect of Gorbachov's new thinking has been to expose a difference of opinion between the NATO partners.

In the longer run, the new thinking has made people wonder about the long-term future of Europe, a continent that until November 1989 had been divided for 40 years by the Berlin Wall. Only now is it beginning to be possible to think of a new Europe, united rather than divided.

In 1989 the USSR withdrew its tanks from Afghanistan. The war had cost many lives and damaged relations with the West.

Gorbachov met Reagan in the Kremlin in May 1988. The Moscow talks helped create a positive atmosphere between the two superpowers.

Gorbachov himself has hinted at the shape of such a Europe, in his frequent references to the 'Common European Home'. In a speech to the Council of Europe in Strasbourg on 6 July 1989, he declared that Europeans can meet the challenges of the coming century only by pooling their efforts. 'We are convinced that what they need is one Europe – peaceful and democratic, a Europe that maintains all its diversity and common humanistic ideas, a prosperous Europe that extends its hand to the rest of the world, a Europe that confidently advances into the future. It is in such a Europe that we visualize our own future.'

Early in December 1989, Presidents Gorbachov and Bush had their first summit meeting, two days of discussion aboard US and Soviet Navy ships in the Mediterranean. Bush had been reluctant to meet Gorbachov before there were any substantial agreements to be signed, but the dramatic developments in Eastern Europe, with the collapse of the authority of the Communist Parties in Hungary, Poland and East Germany, persuaded him that a meeting would be worthwhile.

Many obstacles still stand in the way between the East and West, but the events which are now taking place in Eastern Europe will play a vital role in how future relations will work: the attitude of the Soviet empire to its dependent nations has never been more significant. It is the future of that empire that we will now turn to.

6 The Soviet empire

The Soviet Union survives as the world's last imperial power. But for how much longer? As the French philosopher Alexis de Tocqueville remarked, a despotic system is never at greater risk of collapse than the moment at which it begins to reform.

The Soviet empire inherited by Gorbachov has three distinct components.

First, there are the nations and republics which fall within the Soviet Union proper, including those bequeathed to the Soviet state by the tsars: they include the Ukraine, Byelorussia, the Caucasus, Georgia, Armenia and Azerbaijan. The Soviet Union covers about a sixth of the world's land mass, and includes about 100 different nationalities; but only 50 per cent of its 285 million people are Russians.

Then there are the nations of Eastern Europe that fell helpless into Stalin's hands at the end of the Second World War: Poland, Czechoslovakia, Hungary, East Germany, Bulgaria and Romania. The last two, Yugoslavia and Albania remain Communist but have struck an independent course that has taken them out of Moscow's reach.

The Soviet republics produce many different goods. Sunny Georgia provides fruit, wine and thousands of tonnes of tea.

Finally, there are the nations of the Developing Countries, scenes of the violent conflict of interests between the Communist Soviet Union and the capitalist USA. Behind the American resistance to Soviet influence in these places lay the 'domino theory', which stated that the conversion of one state to Communism would swiftly be followed by the conversion of neighbouring states.

The most important of these nations is Cuba, less than 160 km from the US coast

These UNITA guerillas in Angola have fought a long and bitter war against the government.

and with a unique strategic importance. The others include Vietnam, Angola, Mozambique and Ethiopia. Never part of the empire proper, they are less directly affected by the new climate – though Cuba may yet find that its generous Soviet subsidy ($10 million a day) is cut as austerity begins to bite.

The shadow of somebody hitting the Berlin Wall. The divide between East and West is now disintegrating, creating the prospect of a reunited Germany.

Eastern Europe

In the past, the Soviet Union has intervened militarily to prevent individual nations from taking their own course (Hungary in 1956, Czechoslovakia in 1968), and in 1968 Brezhnev attempted to justify this latter invasion in a speech in Warsaw to the Congress of the Polish Communist Party. Where Communist rule was threatened in one socialist country, he declared, it was the duty of the entire socialist community to avert this threat by whatever means was necessary. The 'Brezhnev Doctrine' meant that the Soviet Union would use force to prevent any of its satellites escaping.

Today the Brezhnev Doctrine is dead. In August 1989, the first non-Communist government in Eastern Europe took office in Poland, led by Tadeusz Mazowiecki, a member of the independent trade union Solidarity. Faced with the utter failure of their policies, and the contempt of the Polish people, the Communist Party was forced to give way, though it retained several important ministries – and control of the police and the army – as part of the Solidarity-led coalition. The Soviet Union, while hardly happy at the eclipse of its sister party in Poland, did nothing.

Hungary is following rapidly along the same course. Multi-party elections are promised in which it is quite possible the Communist Party will be defeated, even though the Hungarian opposition is less well organized than Solidarity in Poland.

Until the autumn of 1989, East Germany had been regarded as the last bastion of Stalinist orthodoxy. But then, in a few dramatic weeks, the situation was transformed. A flood of East German citizens leaving for the West through Hungary and Czechoslovakia, and a series of huge demonstrations in the major cities, led finally to the overthrow of the Communist Party leader Erich Honecker and to his replacement by Egon Krenz. In a desperate – and ultimately unsuccessful – bid to recapture popularity, Krenz promised reforms which included the freedom to travel, and democratic elections. On 10 November, to the astonishment of his citizens, Krenz opened the borders between East and West Germany, knocking holes in the hated Berlin Wall which had kept the two halves of the city divided since 1961. In a single weekend one of the most extraordinary events in modern European history took place. More than two million East Germans – over 10 per cent of the population – crossed the borders to see what life was like on the other side. Amid scenes of intense emotion and joy, families were reunited and new friendships made as the German people mingled freely for the first time in nearly 30 years.

By the end of 1989, two more Communist dictatorships had fallen. In Czechoslovakia, two weeks of demonstrations by hundreds of thousands of people forced the government to resign. Vaclav Havel, the playwright and leading campaigner for human rights, became President barely a year after his last spell in prison. In Romania, an uprising against the dictatorship of Nicolai Ceaucescu became a revolution when the army deserted him. Both Ceaucescu and his wife Elena were executed by a firing squad, and the National Salvation Front, a group pledged to reform and free elections, took office.

The truth is that today Eastern Europe is no longer a bloc in any meaningful sense of the word. Gorbachov has so far stood aloof from the political earthquake in Eastern Europe, while Shevardnadze has said that he could imagine no occasion in which Soviet troops might intervene there. But neither can take the same calm attitude towards the unrest within the Soviet borders, which has already claimed more than 100 lives and is seriously threatening to tear the country apart.

Unwilling to wait for Gorbachov's law on secession, in 1990 Lithuania declared itself independent.

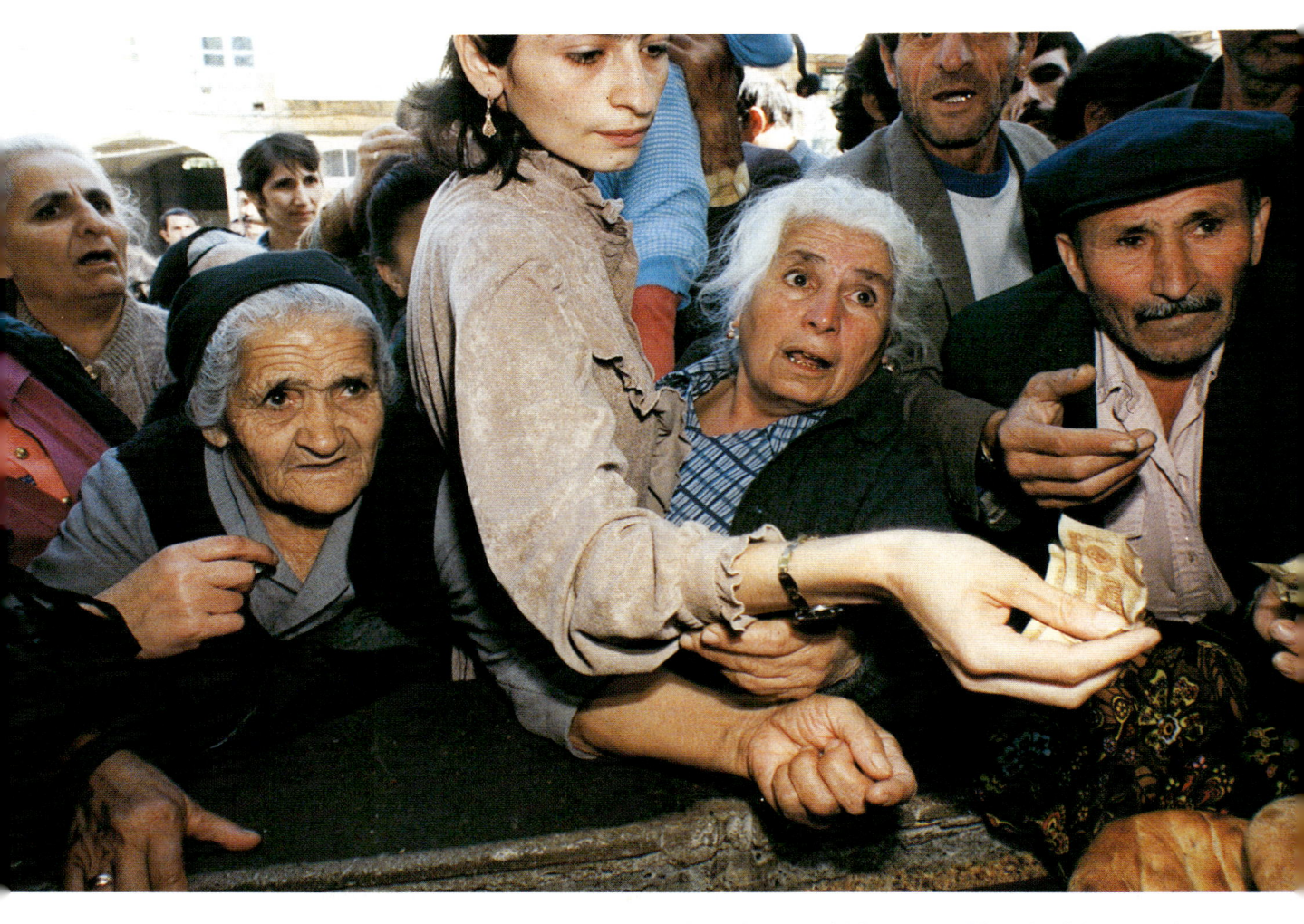

Soviet unrest

The arguments are over language, culture, religion, national identity, and the environment. Some are inter-communal, while others unite the local population against rule from Moscow. Since the end of 1986 they have been breaking out all over the Soviet Union; no sooner is peace restored in some distant province than it is shattered in another.

'In a house in Russia lives a bear whose mad appetite has no limits.'
Banner carried in a demonstration in Estonia.

Residents of Nagorno-Karabakh queuing for bread, after food shipments to the area had been blocked by Azerbaijanis.

In December 1986, for example, there were riots in Alma-Ata, fomented by Kazakh nationalists protesting at the imposition of the Russian language in their schools. Ukrainians and Byelorussians followed suit, demanding constitutional safeguards to protect their languages. The Baltic state of Lithuania, in a move unrecognized by Moscow, went so far as to declare its independence in 1990. Estonia and Latvia also want to secede and have revived their national flags, protesting openly against rule from Moscow and coming into direct conflict with Gorbachov.

Like the Aral Sea, the Baltic coast suffers from pollution. This notice is warning people away from the water's edge.

Since 1940, when the three Baltic states fell back under Russian domination after twenty years of independence, their populations have been diluted by Russian immigration. Today only 60 per cent of those living in Estonia are natives, the rest mostly Russians, while the percentage of native Latvians in Latvia is barely more than half. Fearing that they would be swamped by the Russian immigrants, the Estonians passed an election law in 1988 that deprived many non-Estonians of the vote. This provoked a week of rioting by Russians living in Estonia, and the Kremlin declared the law unconstitutional. In an attempt to control the ferment, in August 1989 the Soviet leadership proposed substantial increases in the rights of autonomous republics and regions. The Kremlin admitted that the 'administrative command system' from Moscow had failed, and that the nationalities question had become 'extremely acute'. A full session of the Party's Central Committee on the issue took place in February 1990.

On March 11 1990, Lithuania declared itself independent. Gorbachov reacted by imposing sanctions on the republic: by not waiting for the legal route to independence, Lithuania's actions had called

Latvians march through their capital, Riga, November 1989, to mark the anniversary of their nation's independence, ended by Soviet occupation. Like Lithuania, Latvia wants to secede.

Gorbachov's authority into serious question. Meanwhile, trouble continued to rumble in Azerbaijan in the bloodiest conflict so far. Old animosities between Armenians and Azerbaijanis flared over the status of a mountainous piece of territory called Nagorno-Karabakh, an enclave within Azerbaijan but largely populated by Armenians. The Armenians demanded control of it, but the Kremlin came down on the Azerbaijani side. In a series of riots in both republics at least 100 people lost their lives. In January 1990, Gorbachov sent in Soviet troops to try to restore order, after Azerbaijani nationalists attacked Armenians and cut off Nagorno-Karabakh. Many were killed as the army forced its way into Baku, the capital of Azerbaijan.

A common thread through many of the regional disturbances is local anger at the damage done to the environment by centrally-planned development. Nowhere is this stronger than in Uzbekistan and Turkmenia, two Muslim republics colonized by Russia a century ago. The planners in

> 'Today we are reaping the fruit of lawlessness in past decades – the deportation of whole peoples from their lands and the burying in oblivion of the national interests of small ethnic groups.' *Mikhail Gorbachov, during a TV address on inter-ethnic problems, 1 July 1989.*

Moscow decreed that the area should be used to grow cotton, at the expense of everything else. For years, huge quantities of fertilizer, pesticide and defoliants have been poured on to the cotton fields, while water has been taken from the two main rivers of the area for irrigation. The Aral Sea, into which the rivers flow, is literally drying up, and the salt and chemicals left behind on the mudflats on its fringes are picked up by winds and swept across the country to poison millions of acres of land.

The scale of the catastrophe is hard to exaggerate. The Aral Sea has fallen by about 15 m in the past 30 years, and its area has shrunk by half. Fishing villages which once lined its shores are now between 32 km and 80 km inland. The health of the local people is miserable.

Though by far the worst example, the ecological disaster in Soviet Central Asia is not unique. The people of the Ukraine are bitterly resentful about the nuclear disaster at Chernobyl, while Siberians protest at the pollution of the world's biggest reservoir of fresh water, Lake Baikal, by a paper mill built on its shores.

A pressure cooker of nationalist unrest is building up which Gorbachov will have to devise some means of controlling. If he does not, it is hard to see the Soviet Union surviving intact into the twenty-first century.

In the lead-up to Lithuania's declaration of independence, and facing similiar demands from republics such as Moldavia, Latvia, Estonia, Georgia and Azerbaijan, Gorbachov proposed a new law providing a mechanism for a republic to leave the Soviet Union. The shortfall between the people's expectations and the actual extent of the changes is the cause of much frustration.

The force of recent events, however, led to the acceptance in March 1990 of a whole package of radical ideas. Among these were the Communist Party's plans to give up its constitutional monopoly of power and compete for its place in government along with other parties. By mid-April the Soviet Communist Party looked set to split into three factions: Boris Yeltsin's and Yuri Afanasyev's Democratic Platform, the Gorbachov-led centre and Ligachov's conservatives.

In the meantime, in an historic vote, Gorbachov was elected President of the USSR by the People's Congress. He was given 'the necessary powers to speed up perestroika', and even to declare a state of emergency if need be.

One thing is certain: if Moscow is to regain control of its subject peoples and to stave off internal unrest it will require either dazzling political skill or the iron fist. For the sake of Gorbachov's reforms, it had better be the former.

Altering the Romanian flag: what is the future for Soviet Communism?

Glossary

Autonomous Self-governing.
Bankruptcy When an organization or person cannot pay its debts.
Bloc A group of states with common interests. The group is bound by an agreement to cooperate.
Bolshevik The majority group in the Russian Social Democratic Party who followed the lead of Lenin after the party split in 1903. The minority were called Mensheviks.
Bureaucrat An office worker, civil servant or functionary of the state.
Capitalism Competitive, economic system in which businesses are owned by individuals or by groups of individuals.
Censors Officials who determine what may or may not be published.
Class struggle A Marxist concept stating that history is determined by a battle between different social classes.
Collectivization Division of land into very large farms owned by the state and worked by teams of laborers.
Command economy Economy controlled by orders from a central government organization.
Communism Society in which all property is collectively owned and where labor is organized for the common good. So far, the societies that we call "Communist" have not achieved true communism but instead are in a state of socialism.
Cooperatives Private businesses run by a few people working together.
Coup d'etat Military seizure of power.
Demographer Expert on population.
Demokratizatsiya Democratization, or working for the principle of government by the people for the people.
Dictat Command that must be obeyed.
Dissident One who disagrees with orthodox thinking.
Entrepreneur A person in business who takes risks in order to make profits.

Faction Small group within a political party.
Fascism Nationalist political theory followed by Adolf Hitler and Italian dictator Benito Mussolini.
Glasnost Openness.
Ideology A set of ideas firmly held and used to determine policy or behaviour.
Insurrection Armed rising against authority.
Iron Curtain Division of Europe between socialist East and capitalist West; border between the two blocs.
Joint venture Business enterprise between two companies sharing costs and profits.
Komsomol Youth branch of the Soviet Communist Party.
Labour camps Prisons, usually in remote areas, where criminals and political prisoners are sent to work.
Liberation struggle The effort of poor countries to free themselves from domination or colonization by the rich.
Marxist Person who accepts Karl Marx's analysis of society.
Mausoleum Stately burial place.
NATO The North Atlantic Treaty Organization. The military alliance which is made up of Belgium, Britain, Canada, Denmark, France, Greece, Iceland, Italy, Luxembourg, the Netherlands, Norway, Portugal, Spain, Turkey, the USA and West Germany.
Nazi-Soviet Pact Agreement signed in 1939 between the Soviet Union and Nazi Germany, by which Stalin sought to avoid war. Despite the agreement, Hitler attacked in 1941.
People's Congress The Soviet parliament.
Perestroika Gorbachov's programme of reform.
Politburo The inner cabinet of the Soviet Communist Party.
Proletariat Working class.
Supreme Soviet Smaller Soviet Parliament

selected from members of the People's Congress.

Tsar Ruler of Russia before revolution; king.

Vanguard The people at the head or front of a movement, in this case the Communist Party.

Books to read

Aganbegyan, Abel, *The Challenge: Economics of Perestroika* (Hutchinson Education, 1988)

Binyon, Michael, *Life in Russia* (Hamish Hamilton, 1983)

Brzezinski, Zbigniew, *The Grand Failure* (Scribners, New York, 1989)

Frankel, Joseph, *International Relations in a Changing World* (Oxford University Press, 1988)

Gorbachov, Mikhail, *Perestroika* (Collins, 1987)

Hingley, Ronald, *A Concise History of Russia* (Thames & Hudson, 1972)

Kaiser, Robert G., *Russia, the People and the Power* (Secker and Warburg, 1976)

Medvedev, Zhores A., *Gorbachov* (Penguin, 1986)

Sakharov, Andrei D., *My Country and the World* (Collins & Harvill Press, 1975)

Further information

If you wish to find out more about some of the subjects covered in this book, you might find the following addresses useful:

United Kingdom

Komsomol
50 Bell House
Warwick Road
London W14

Novosti Press Agency
3 Rosary Gardens
London SW7

USA

Tass
50 Rockefeller Plaza
Suite 501
N.Y. 10020

USSR

Komsomol
Pravda 24
Moscow

Tass
P.O. 100
Moscow
USSR

Picture acknowledgements

Camera Press COVER, 8, 10, 17, 37, 38; Chapel Studios 12, 14, 25; George Coles 40; Novosti 11, 16, 21, 22, 24, 27; Photo Co-op 20; Rex Features frontispiece, 18, 32, 33 (top), 41, 43, 45; Tass 13, 28, 30, 31 (left); Topham 6, 7, 9, 23, 26, 29, 31 (right), 33 (bottom), 35, 36, 39, 42, 44. The artwork on page 15 is by Malcolm Walker.

Index

Afghanistan 34, 36
Agriculture 8, 10, 13, 17, 18, 21, 23, 24
Albania 15, 38
Andropov, Yuri 11, 18, 19
Armenia 15, 33, 38, 44
Azerbaijan 15, 33, 38, 42, 44, 45

Baltic states 33, 42, 43
Berlin Wall 36, 40, 41
Brezhnev, Leonid 10, 11, 14, 18, 28, 31, 34, 40
Britain 6, 18, 34, 35, 36
Bulgaria 15, 38
Bush, George 37
Byelorussia 15, 38, 42

Capitalism 6, 10, 39
Ceaucescu, Nicolai 33, 41
Chernenko, Konstantin 11, 18
Command economy 9, 19, 44
Communist Party 7, 10, 11, 14, 16, 17, 24, 26, 27, 28, 30, 31, 37, 38, 40, 41, 43, 45
Communist Party Congress 10, 17, 40
Cuba 10, 11, 36, 39
Czechoslovakia 15, 38, 40, 41

Decentralization 10
Democratization 28, 33
Demonstrations 26, 29, 33, 40
Détente 10, 34
Dissidents 7, 31

East Germany 15, 37, 38, 40, 41
Estonia 15, 32, 33, 42, 43, 45
Europe 12, 13, 34, 35, 36, 37, 40
  East 14, 36, 37, 38, 40, 41
  West 23, 36, 37

Georgia 15, 33, 35, 38, 45
Gorbachov, Mikhail 9, 11, 12, 13, 14, 45

glasnost 27–33, 34
international relations 34–45
perestroika 19–26, 27, 29, 30, 31, 32, 34, 45
rise of 16–18
Gosplan 19, 21, 25
Gromyko, Andrei 35

Hungary 15, 37, 38, 40

Importation of goods 12, 13
Inter-Regional Group 31

KGB 7, 32
Khrushchev, Nikita 10, 11, 17, 28
Komsomol 16, 17
Kremlin 13, 14, 26, 37, 43, 44

Latvia 15, 32, 42, 43, 44, 45
Lenin, Vladimir Ilyich 6, 7, 8, 17, 21, 28, 31, 34
Ligachov, Yegor 30, 32, 45
Lithuania 15, 32, 41, 42
Living standards 14, 20, 25

Marx 6, 7, 19, 36
Media, the 29–31
Moldavia 15, 33, 45
Moscow News 13, 29
Multi-party elections 14, 40, 45

Nagorno-Karabakh 15, 42, 44
NATO 34, 36
New technology 13, 19, 20, 34
New thinking 34
Nixon, Richard 10
Nuclear weapons 10, 11, 12, 31, 34, 35

Ogonyok 29, 30

People's Congress 27, 28, 31, 32, 45
Poland 15, 37, 38, 40
Politburo 11, 16, 18, 24, 28, 30, 32, 42
Pollution 14, 29, 43, 44

Pravda 30
Private enterprise 19
Productivity 19

Reagan, Ronald 35, 36, 37
Reforms 10, 11, 23, 24, 28, 30, 31
Romania 15, 33, 38, 41, 45

Sakharov, Andrei 28, 31
Shevardnadze, Eduard 34, 35, 41
Socialism 6, 23, 40
Solzhenitsyn, Alexander 29
Soviet
  economy 9, 10, 12, 13, 14, 19, 21, 24, 35
  foreign trade 21
  industry 9, 10, 12, 13, 19, 20, 25, 26
  republics 14, 38
Space exploration 12
Stalin 7, 8, 9, 10, 11, 12, 13, 14, 16, 17, 28, 29, 30, 31, 33, 38, 40
State
  budget 14, 21
  enterprises 24
Strikes 26
Supreme Soviet 27, 30

Thatcher, Margaret 36
Turkmenia 15, 44

Ukraine 15, 33, 38, 42, 44
United Nations 34
USA 7, 10, 11, 12, 13, 14, 19, 21, 34, 35, 39
Uzbekistan 15, 33, 44

Vietnam 11, 39

Wages 24
Western
  economy 21
  influence 28
West Germany 34, 36, 40, 41
Workers 6, 7, 9
World league 14

Yeltsin, Boris 28, 32, 45
Yugoslavia 15, 38